POP PERFORMANCE PIECES

Clarinet & Piano

T0078979

Published by
Chester Music
part of The Music Sales Group
14-15 Berners Street,
London W1T 3LJ, UK.

Exclusive Distributors:
Music Sales Limited
Distribution Centre, Newmarket Road,
Bury St Edmunds, Suffolk IP33 3YB, UK.
Music Sales Pty Limited
Level 4, Lisgar House,
30-32 Carrington Street,
Sydney, NSW 2000 Australia.

Order No. CH85052
ISBN 978-1-78558-333-9

Piano scores are transposed.
Chord symbols at concert pitch.

Clarinet consultant: Howard McGill.
Piano consultant: Lisa Cox.
Compiled and edited by Naomi Cook.
Music formatted by Sarah Lofthouse, SEL Music Art Ltd.

Photographs courtesy of Ruth Keating,
assisted by Lisa Cox and James Welland.
Special thanks to the pupils at St Benedict's School, Ealing
and their Director of Music Christopher Eastwood for taking
part in the photo shoot.

Printed in the EU.

Your Guarantee of Quality
As publishers, we strive to produce every book to
the highest commercial standards. This book has
been carefully designed to minimise awkward
page turns and to make playing from it a real
pleasure. Particular care has been given to
specifying acid-free, neutral-sized paper made
from pulps which have not been elemental chlorine
bleached. This pulp is from farmed sustainable
forests and was produced with special regard for
the environment. Throughout, the printing and
binding have been planned to ensure a sturdy,
attractive publication which should give years
of enjoyment.If your copy fails to meet our high
standards, please inform us and we will gladly
replace it.

www.musicsales.com

&

CHESTER MUSIC
part of The Music Sales Group
London / New York / Paris / Sydney / Copenhagen / Berlin / Madrid / Hong Kong / Tokyo

ALL OF ME

Words & Music by John Legend & Tobias Gad

Hints & Tips: Make sure you use the dynamics to help build interest in the piece, being careful not to overpower the melody. There are many held notes throughout — resist the urge to rely on the pedal to sustain the notes rather than holding them for their full value. Practise without the pedal first!

Soulful ballad ♩ = 126

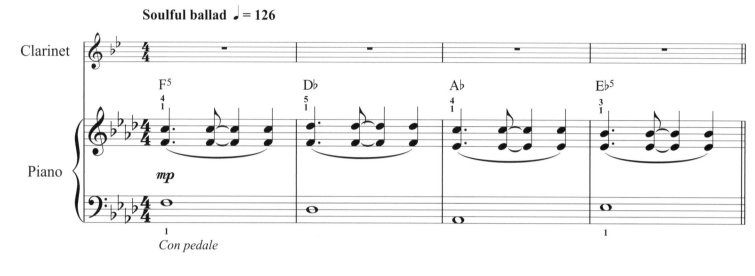

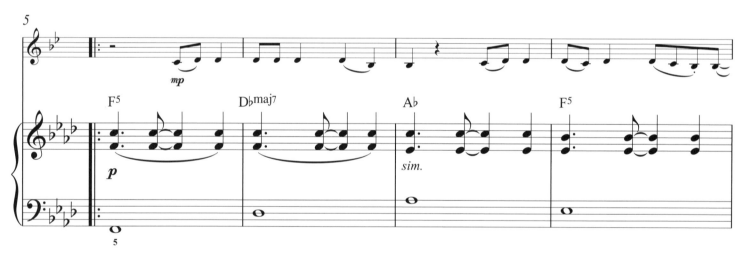

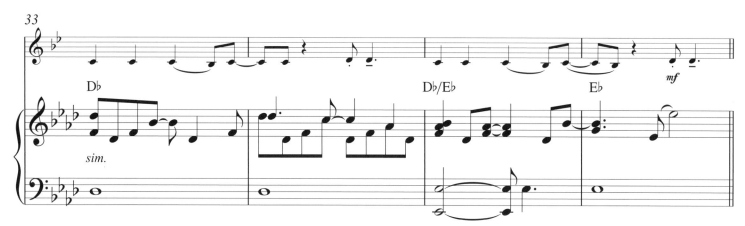

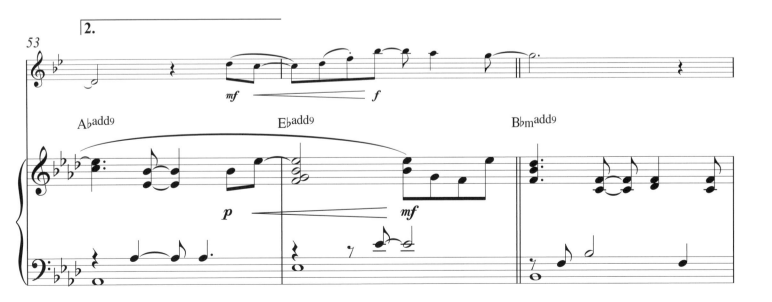

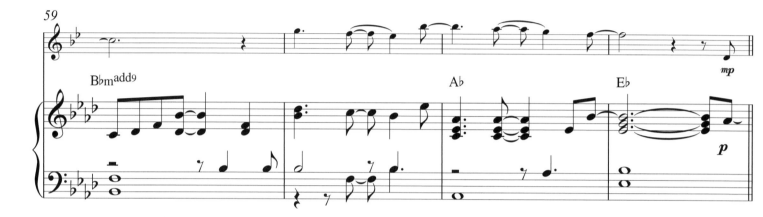

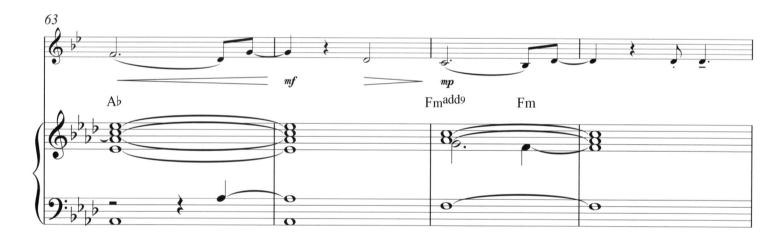

D.S. al Coda

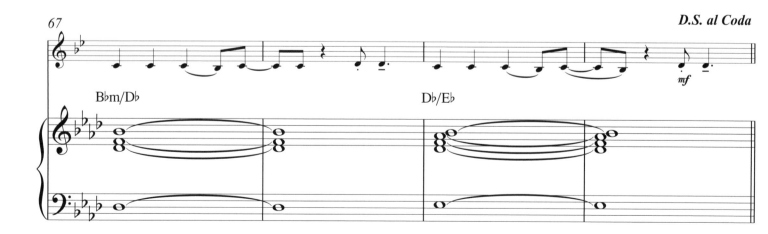

BRIDGE OVER TROUBLED WATER

Words & Music by Paul Simon

Hints & Tips: There are lots of block chords in this piece: make sure you use the correct fingers in anticipation of the next chord position. Watch out for the accidentals too!

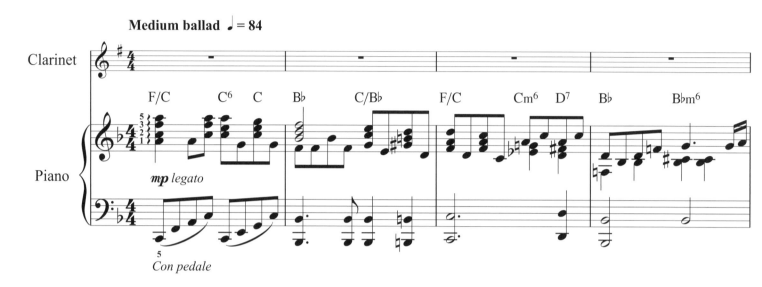

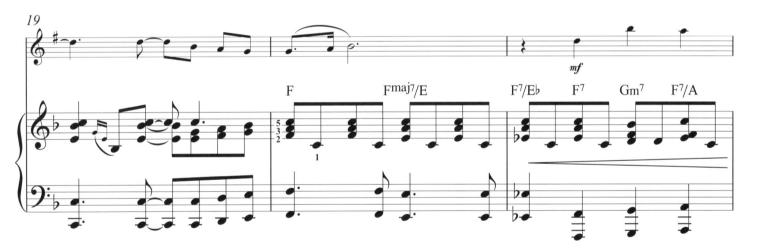

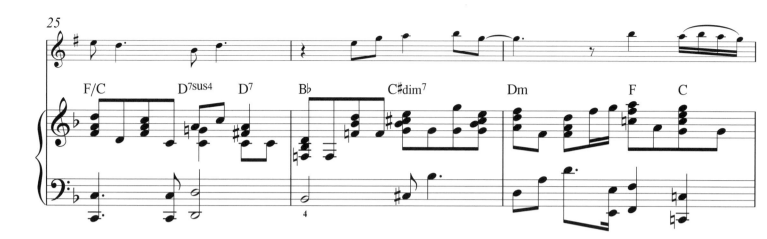

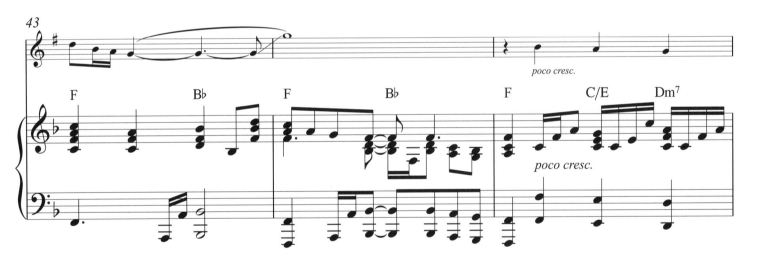

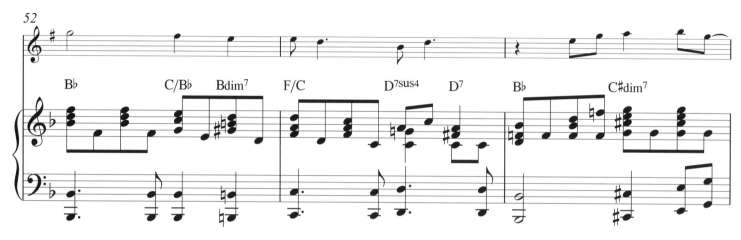

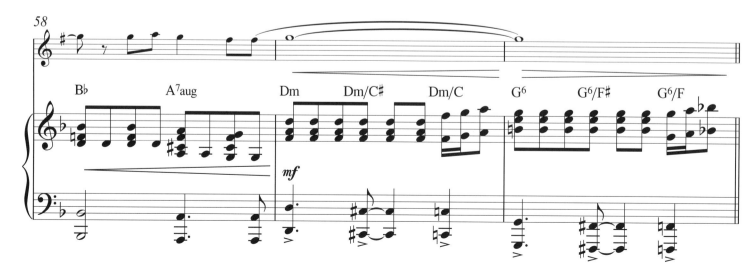

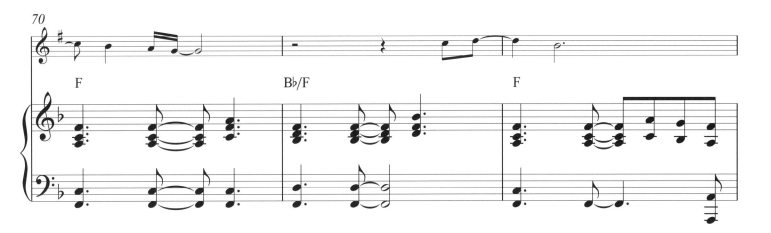

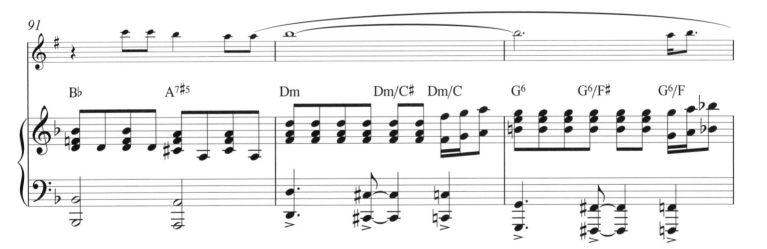

CLOCKS

Words & Music by Guy Berryman, Jonathan Buckland,
William Champion & Christopher Martin

Hints & Tips: Keep the left hand crisp and on the beat and pay attention to keeping a steady pulse. From bar 53 there is a repeated quaver pattern in the right hand played with the 5th finger — make sure the quavers are even as this finger can get tired quite quickly.

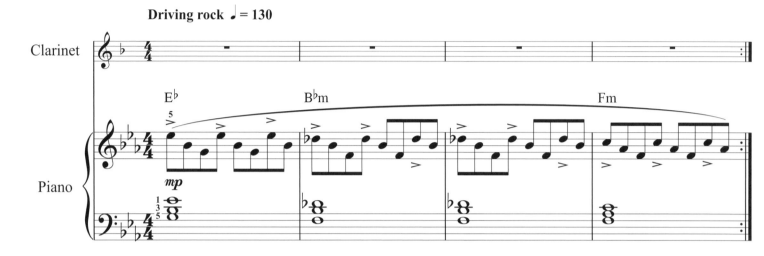

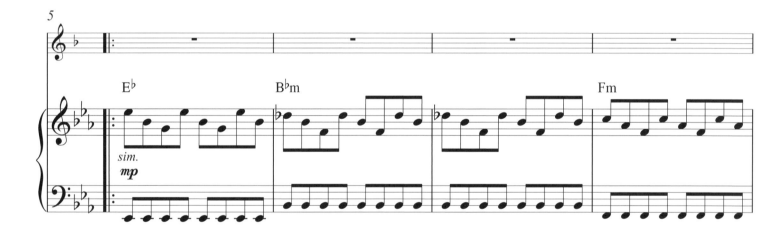

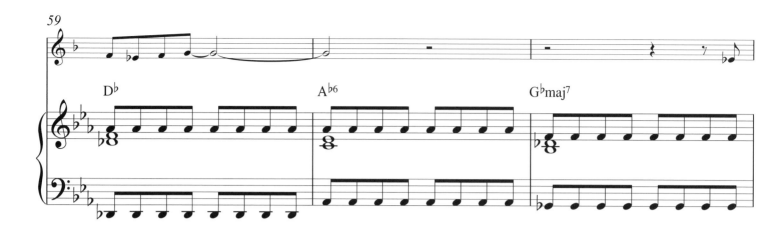

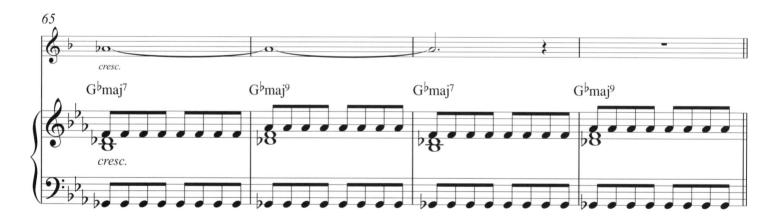

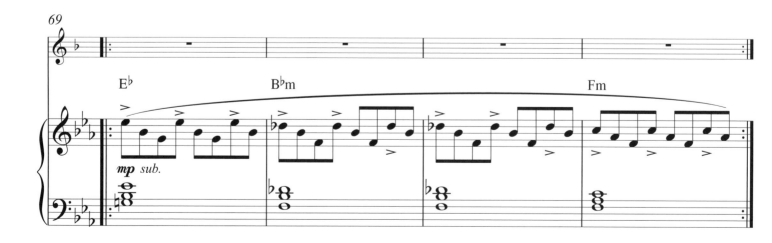

DON'T STOP BELIEVIN'

Words & Music by Steve Perry, Neal Schon & Jonathan Cain

Hints & Tips: Bring out the famous bass line in the left hand and watch out for the off-beat rhythms — make sure you count carefully to ensure every note falls in the right place. Work with the soloist to ensure you play your shared rhythms exactly together in the chorus (e.g. bars 41 and 42).

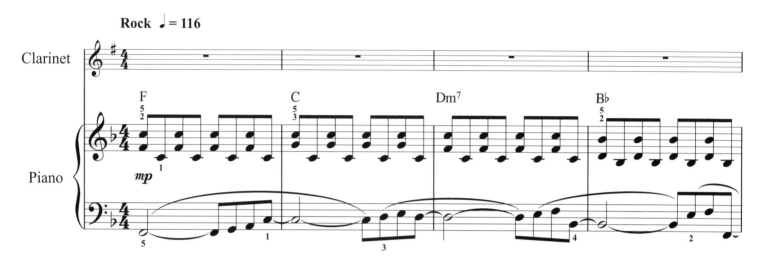

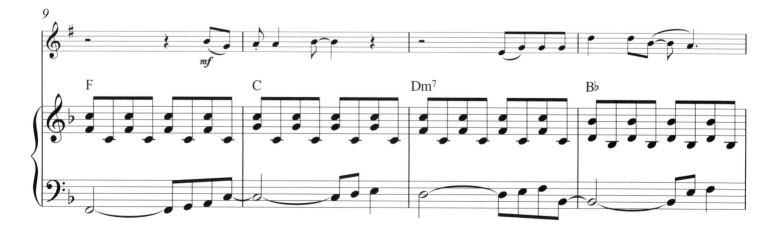

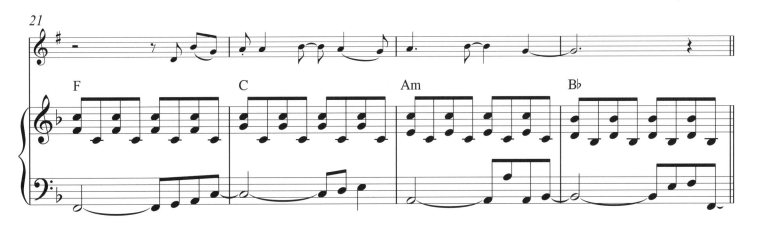

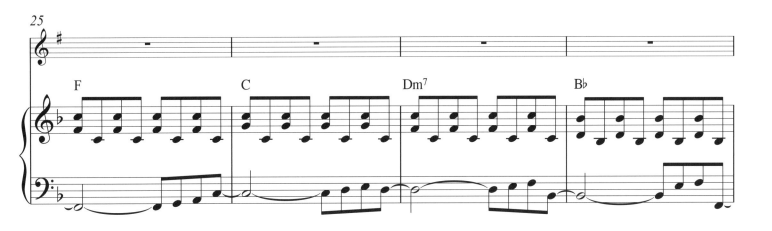

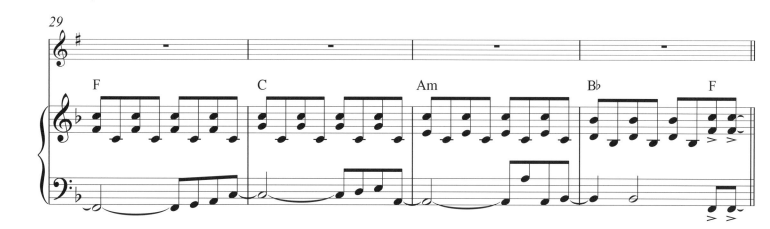

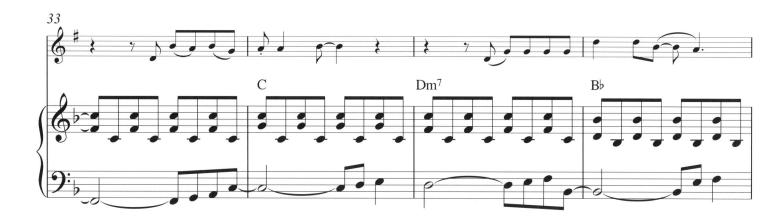

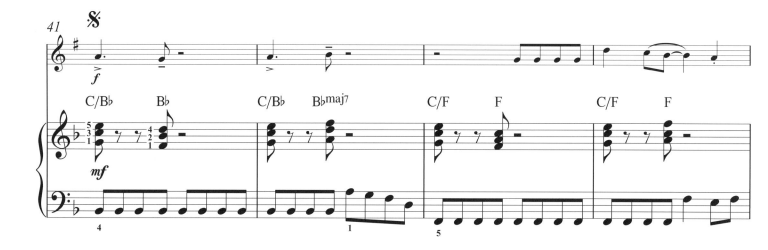

To Coda ⊕

Coda

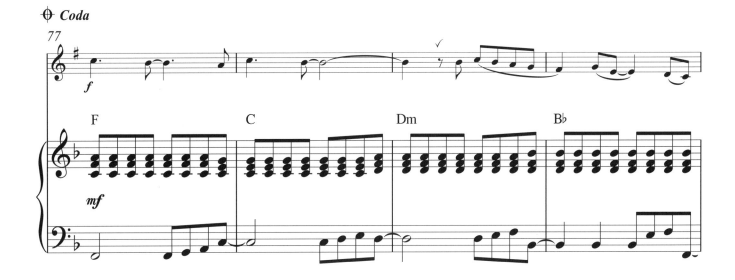

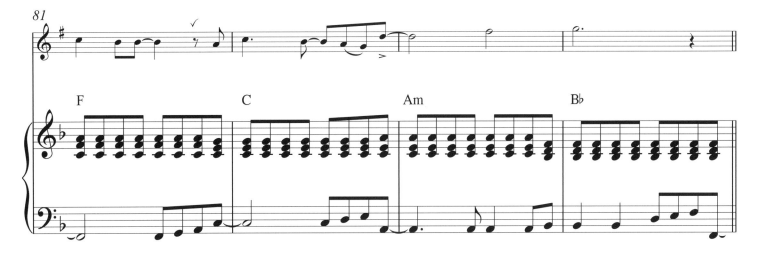

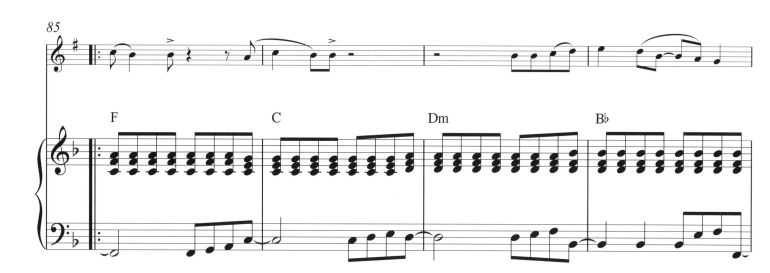

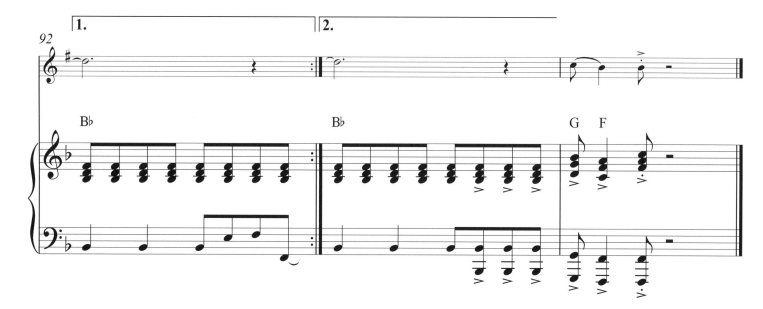

POP PERFORMANCE PIECES

Published by
Chester Music
part of The Music Sales Group
14-15 Berners Street,
London W1T 3LJ, UK.

Exclusive Distributors:
Music Sales Limited
Distribution Centre, Newmarket Road,
Bury St Edmunds, Suffolk IP33 3YB, UK.
Music Sales Pty Limited
Level 4, Lisgar House,
30-32 Carrington Street,
Sydney, NSW 2000 Australia.

Order No. CH85052
ISBN 978-1-78558-333-9

Piano scores are transposed.
Chord symbols at concert pitch.

Clarinet consultant: Howard McGill.
Piano consultant: Lisa Cox.
Compiled and edited by Naomi Cook.
Music formatted by Sarah Lofthouse, SEL Music Art Ltd.

Photographs courtesy of Ruth Keating,
assisted by Lisa Cox and James Welland.
Special thanks to the pupils at St Benedict's School, Ealing
and their Director of Music Christopher Eastwood for taking
part in the photo shoot.

Printed in the EU.

Your Guarantee of Quality
As publishers, we strive to produce every book to
the highest commercial standards. This book has
been carefully designed to minimise awkward
page turns and to make playing from it a real
pleasure. Particular care has been given to
specifying acid-free, neutral-sized paper made
from pulps which have not been elemental chlorine
bleached. This pulp is from farmed sustainable
forests and was produced with special regard for
the environment. Throughout, the printing and
binding have been planned to ensure a sturdy,
attractive publication which should give years
of enjoyment.If your copy fails to meet our high
standards, please inform us and we will gladly
replace it.

www.musicsales.com

POP PERFORMANCE PIECES

Clarinet Part

CHESTER MUSIC
part of The Music Sales Group
London / New York / Paris / Sydney / Copenhagen / Berlin / Madrid / Hong Kong / Tokyo

ALL OF ME

Words & Music by John Legend & Tobias Gad

Hints & Tips: There are lots of repeated notes in this song; keep them connected with gentle articulation. The pieces starts in the chalumeau register: try to get as warm a sound as possible. The middle eight from bar 54 can really sing out. It's syncopated (played on the off-beats) — make sure you stay in time and don't rush!

BRIDGE OVER TROUBLED WATER

Words & Music by Paul Simon

Hints & Tips: The octave glissando from bar 15 to 16 (and 43 to 44) is a tricky one: try to run up a G major scale as quickly as possible and 'smear' all the notes together. Pay particular attention as you cross over the break. Gershwin's famous 'Rhapsody In Blue' starts with a similar effect.

CLOCKS

Words & Music by Guy Berryman, Jonathan Buckland,
William Champion & Christopher Martin

Hints & Tips: This number should be played with strong rhythmic intensity, giving the crotchets a good accent. Quavers on beat one could be played staccato to emphasise the syncopation. Make sure the B♭ 'throat note' is played with a good tone as this is the weakest note on the clarinet.

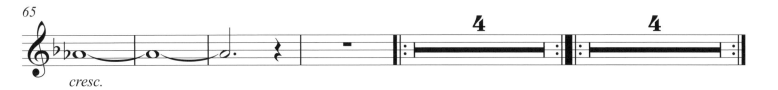

Play 4 times

DON'T STOP BELIEVIN'

Words & Music by Steve Perry, Neal Schon & Jonathan Cain

Hints & Tips: This whole song is played in the middle to low register; try to make it as interesting as possible with contrasting dynamics and clear articulation.

FIREWORK

Words & Music by Tor Erik Hermansen, Katy Perry,
Mikkel S. Eriksen, Sandy Wilhelm & Ester Dean

Hints & Tips: This has quite a simple, repetitive melody so it requires you to deliver it in a musical way, building to bar 13. Let the chorus sing out in the upper register from bar 28. Bars 46, 48, 50 and 70 are great for staccato tongue practice. They are played on the weakest note, B♭ — ask your teacher about alternative fingering.

A THOUSAND MILES

Words & Music by Vanessa Carlton

Hints & Tips: There are some challenging rhythms in this song: keep feeling the semiquaver subdivision all the way through and lock into your very own internal drum machine! Have a think about how you might vary the melody on the repeat from bar 45 — you could ask the pianist to loop bars 45–52 while you try out some ideas.

D.S. al Coda

𝄌 **Coda**

(2° **𝆑**, ad lib. melody)

1.

2.

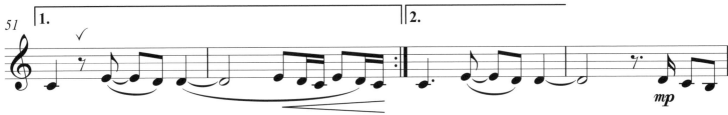

2

A THOUSAND YEARS

Words & Music by David Hodges & Christina Perri

Hints & Tips: This piece has a 12/8 groove, i.e. there are 4 beats in a bar with each one sub-divided into a triplet. This all changes in bar 10, when you have to carefully place a 'two against three'. Try to sing this rhythm to yourself before playing the song. Really let the upper register sing out on the chorus when it goes up the octave (bars 19 and 35).

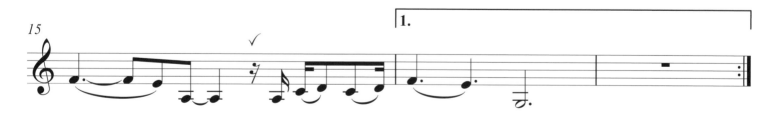

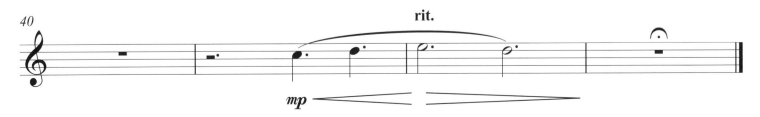

WHEN WE WERE YOUNG

Words & Music by Adele Adkins & Tobias Jesso

Hints & Tips: Make sure you connect the repeated notes at the start of this song. Bars 43 and 44 are great for practising syncopated rhythms. This piece requires some stamina: try to build it up over the course of a week if you feel your lip starting to quiver on the D.S.!

YOUR SONG

Words & Music by Elton John & Bernie Taupin

Hints & Tips: This song is perfect for practising playing smoothly across the break — you need to move a lot of fingers, but we don't want to hear it! Try not to separate the repeated notes too much (e.g. bars 3 and 5).

mf joyfully

cresc.

mp

1.

2.

cresc.

mp

MAD WORLD

Words & Music by Roland Orzabal

Hints & Tips: Try to get evenness across the break (A to B). This is a great song for tonguing practice as it has lots of repeated notes. It's also a good test of rhythmic placement: make sure you don't rush the syncopated notes. Remember to prepare for the D♯ in bar 22 by preceding it with a left hand little finger C♯!

123456789

Chester Music

part of The Music Sales Group

CH85052

www.musicsales.com

FIREWORK

Words & Music by Tor Erik Hermansen, Katy Perry,
Mikkel S. Eriksen, Sandy Wilhelm & Ester Dean

Hints & Tips: Make sure the driving quaver pattern in crisp and clear throughout.
Watch out for the change to off-beat rhythms at bar 45!

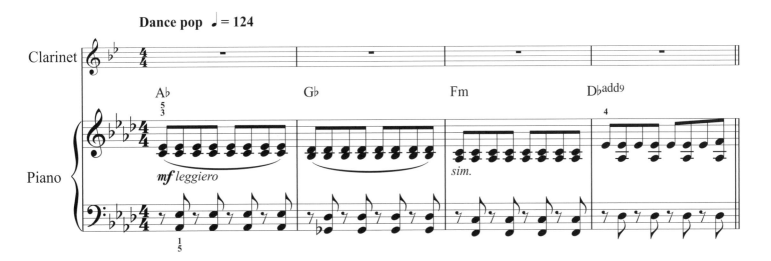

MAD WORLD

Words & Music by Roland Orzabal

Hints & Tips: Make sure the dynamic of the broken chord pattern stays the same when it switches to the right hand in bar 5. Bring out the lovely counter-melody in the right hand at bar 29. The rhythms are less predictable in the right hand from bar 22 — count carefully!

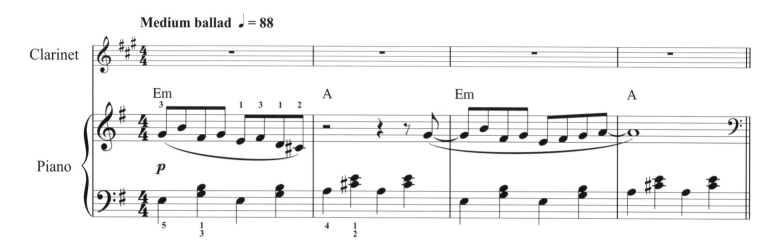

A THOUSAND YEARS

Words & Music by David Hodges & Christina Perri

Hints & Tips: There is a broad range of dynamics in this piece; make sure you make the most of these contrasts.
Practise playing the right hand duplets in bar 11 against the quavers in the left hand until you are secure with
the rhythms. Use the pedal to sustain the block chords in the right hand from bar 23.

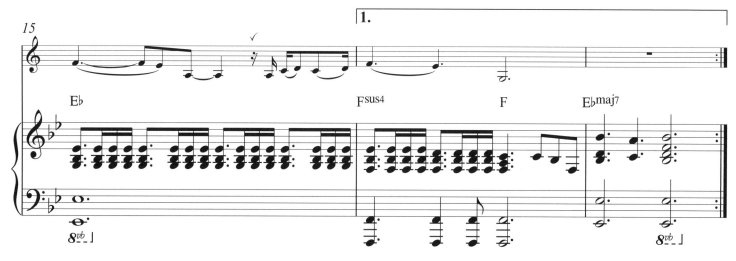

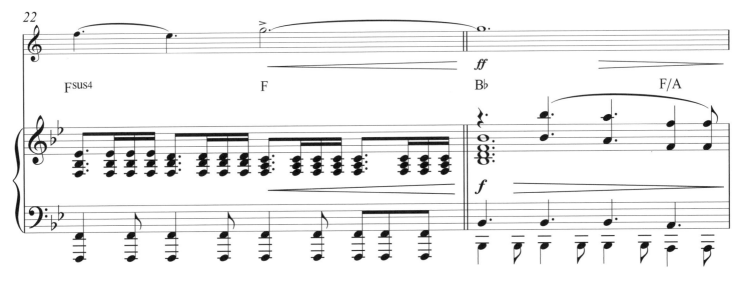

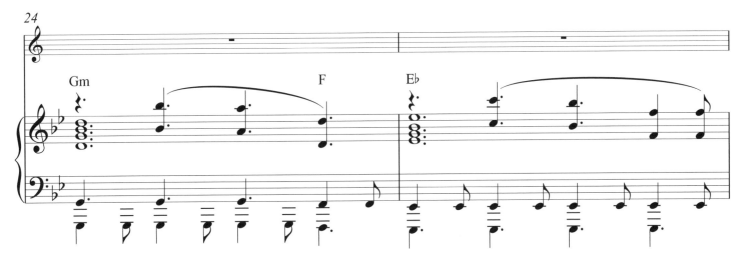

A THOUSAND MILES

Words & Music by Vanessa Carlton

Hints & Tips: This piece features a brilliant piano part! Remember to keep the semiquaver patterns crisp and even. There is a lot of movement in both hands so make sure you're ready for the octave jumps. Practise the call-and-response passages with the soloist (from bars 14 and 40), ensuring you keep to a steady tempo.

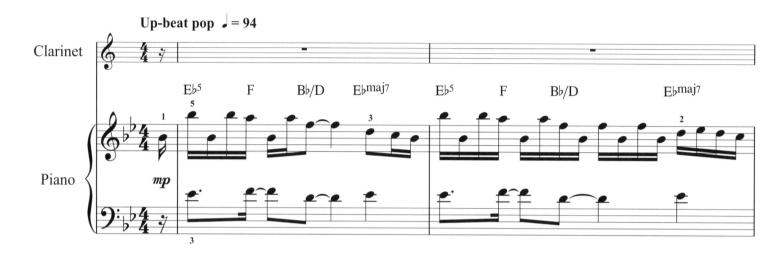

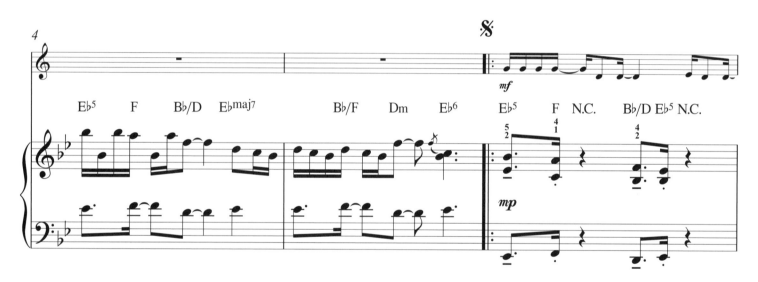

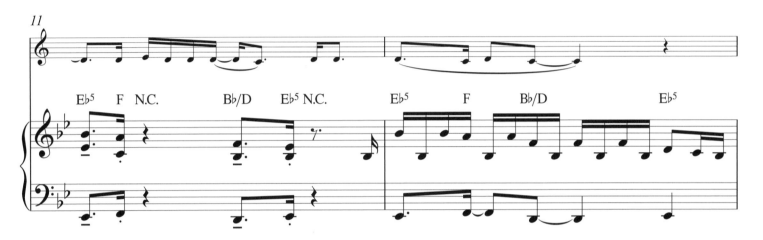

To Coda ⊕

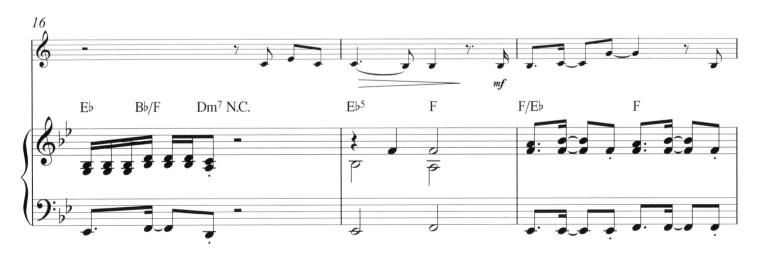

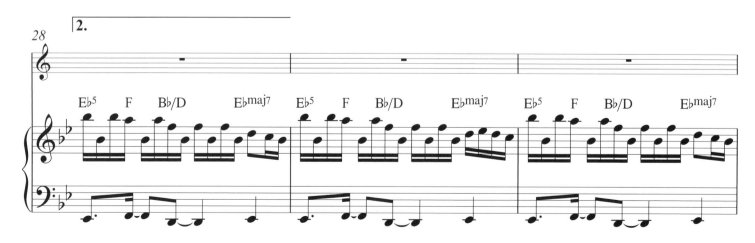

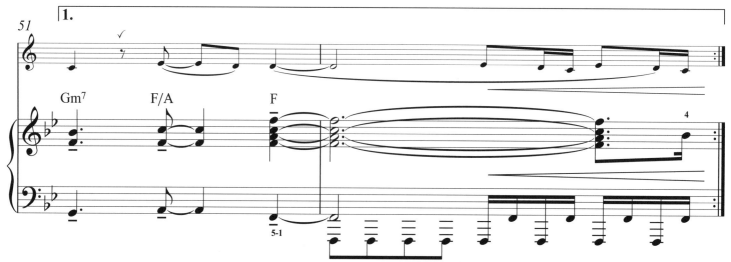

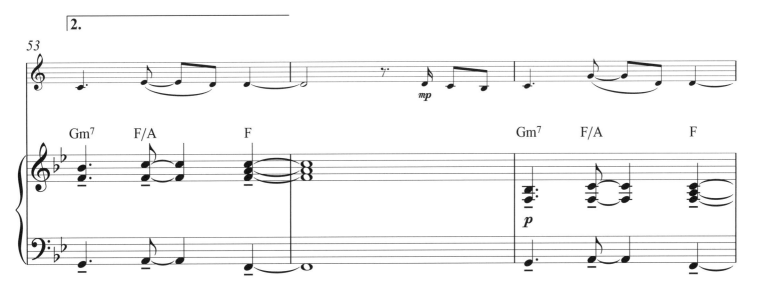

YOUR SONG

Words & Music by Elton John & Bernie Taupin

Hints & Tips: This piano part is quite busy so it's important to be sensitive to the soloist, being careful not to overpower them. Make sure you lift the pedal for every change in harmony so the sound doesn't become muddy. Some of the chords involve big stretches: play all the notes together first to get used to the shapes.

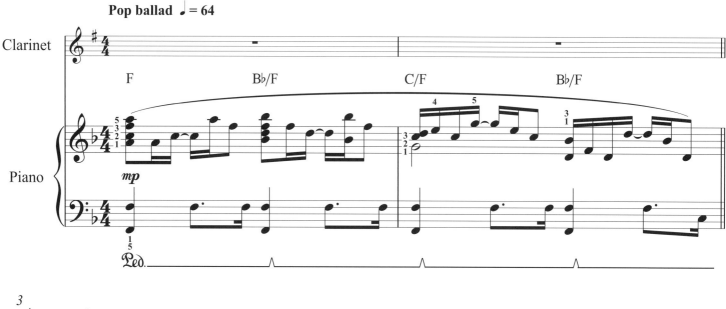

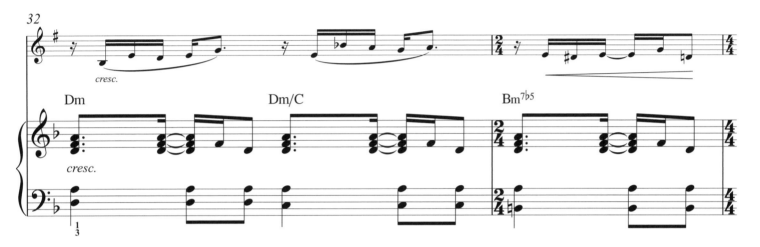

WHEN WE WERE YOUNG

Words & Music by Adele Adkins & Tobias Jesso

Hints & Tips: Work on getting the chord changes as smooth as possible and make sure you feel a steady pulse so you're not tempted to rush the held notes at the start of the piece. If the double octaves in the left hand are too big a stretch, just play the bottom note. Watch out for the big jump in both hands at bar 47!

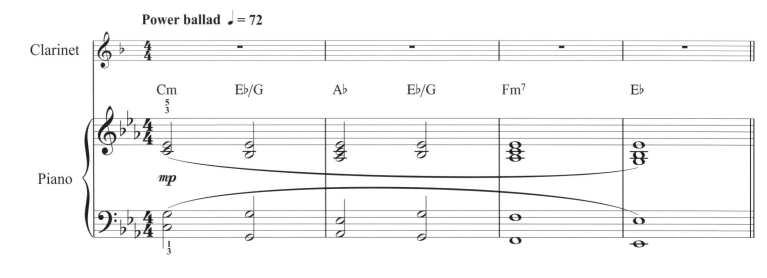

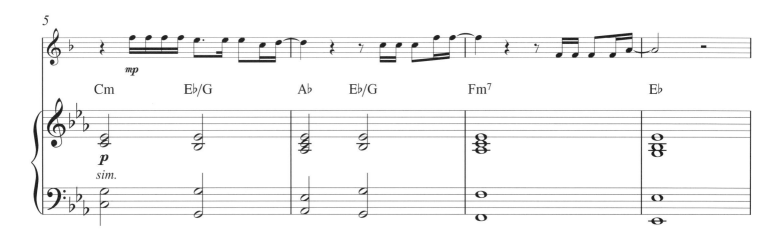

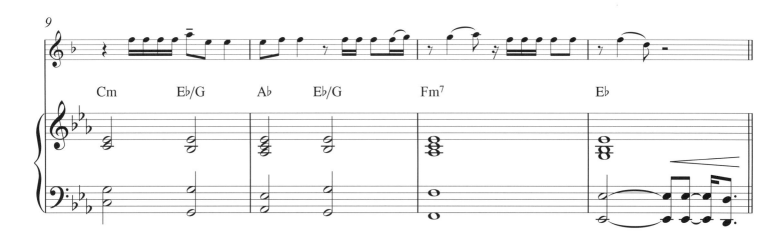

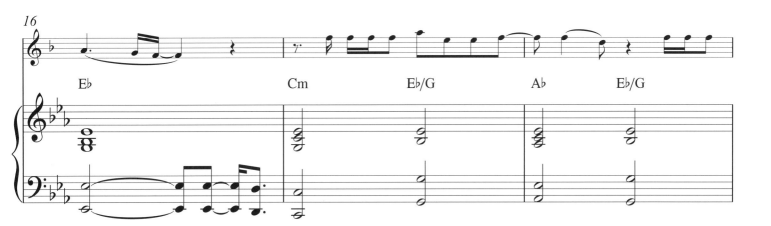

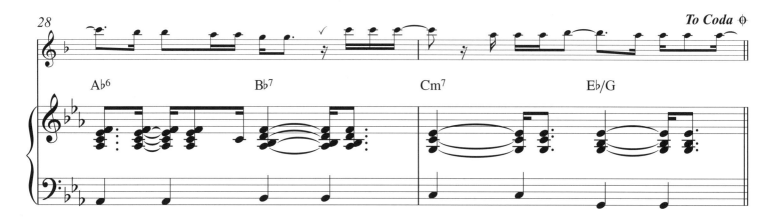

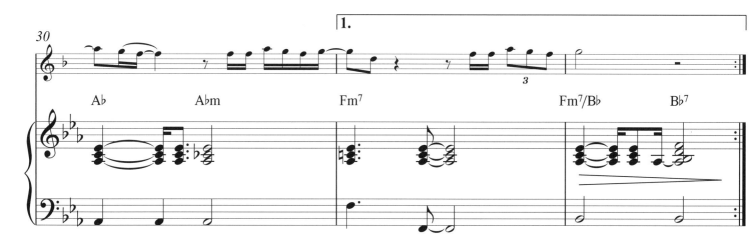

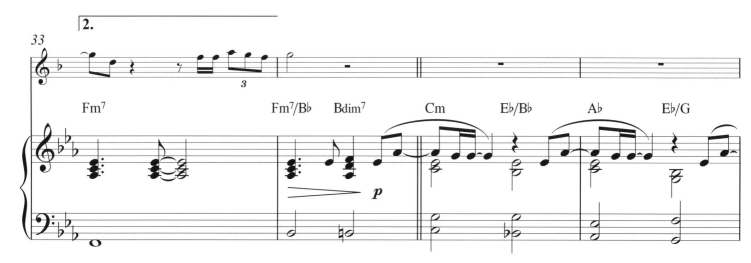

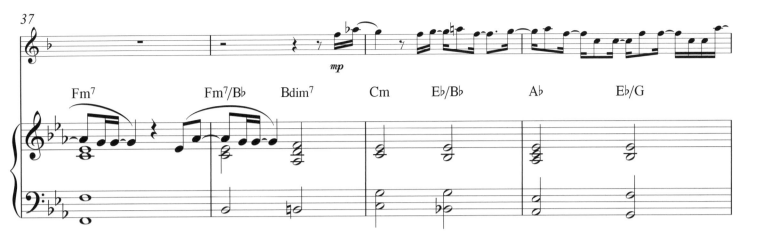

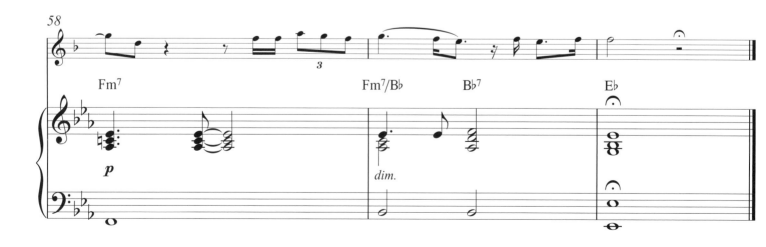

123456789